ON THE WAY TO WHOLENESS

Debbe,

May God bless you

Janet

ON THE WAY TO WHOLENESS

By Way of ACTSS

Janet Genson

To order additional copies of this book, contact:
Xlibris Corporation
1-888-795-4274
www.Xlibris.com
Orders@Xlibris.com
80565

CONTENTS

To Lord Jesus, my Teacher, my Friend. In good times and bad, in sickness and in health, until death do us part. We shall be reunited and know true peace.

To Junior, my wonderful, patient, loving husband, who believed in me before I believed in myself. You are the face of Jesus I get to wake up with each day.

Marilyn and Kathy, you both knew me when . . . You have stayed by my side, encouraged me, and believed in me.

My Couple Connections family, you gave me space to talk, to grow, and to move forward.

Ray L, you made a walk with Jesus real to me. You taught me, loved me like a father, and then sent me on my way.

Nancy, little sister, you showed me what forgiveness looks like, and you loved me in spite of myself.

Dick B, you taught me, our class; and boy, it was a wonderful journey.

PK, we have known each other for years, and all we knew was a surface friendship. As we settled in Virginia, you have stepped beside me and become a close and dear friend. Thank you. You taught me, corrected me, and I learned.

Judy, you took me under your wing when I had the desire but not the skill or courage. You met with me for a few years after work in the hospitality center at church. Thank you for your patience and your wonderful friendship of love as I grew into a writer.

To Xlibris who helped me through with patience and kindness and who made the book possible.

Lastly, our babies—our cats: Alex, Blanko, Sara, and Missy. You have snuggled, played, and loved me when I needed it most.

PREFACE

My parents took me and my siblings to church pretty much each Sunday when we were growing up. Mom and Dad served on the board of deacons and elders and held various other positions within the church. When we were in grade school and junior high school, my siblings and I often helped with weddings by doing dishes, cooking, and setting up the hall in the church. My sister and I sang in the choir. We learned how to fight in sign language and quite frequently had our fights in the choir loft in front of the congregation. I guess that may be why the children's and teen's choirs were relegated to the balcony.

In Sunday school, we learned many lessons about Jesus. As I began a serious faith journey in my forties, I was amazed at what I already knew. In church, I heard flowery prayers. Our church often recited prayers that were printed in the bulletin. I also witnessed my own father's amazing recovery from polio. The doctors did not believe our dad would live. Many adult-onset polio patients did not survive polio. Dad also taught himself how to walk when no one believed he could. Dad talked to our minister and believed he could learn how to walk if he could get a back brace. The church provided a back brace for Dad. When Mom was at work and us kids were in school, Dad worked on learning how to walk. Sometimes, he would fall, and it took him a long time to pull himself to the wheelchair and get back in. Dad eventually did walk. He walked funny, looked like a drunk at times, but he walked on his own two feet. When Dad went upstairs, he had to bend over almost in half and hold on to a rail, but he got himself up the stairs.

Our church was wonderful; they provided food, clothes, and even helped Mom get a mortgage. Back in the 1960s, women could not get mortgages easily. First, Grandma's job in a hospital cafeteria would send food home and then our church helped us. As our family became more self-sufficient, we then began to give back to the church. We were grateful for all the wonderful help we received.

With all this loving support, I did not figure out how to have a personal relationship with Jesus. My prayers were sporadic and halfhearted attempts to talk to God. I spent many years wondering who the Holy Spirit was and wondered why I needed to pray in Jesus's name. I felt like, "Why go to the middleman? Why not go directly to God?"

As with every generation before us, each must find God and accept Him as their own. It is not a given right that we will be saved if our parents were Christians, we go to church, or do nice things. We can't work our way into heaven. We have to accept Jesus, the gift of the cross, and allow ourselves to be transformed by God. For me, as I began my faith journey, I was given the ACTSS prayer format by a Christian counselor. As I prayed this prayer format, I began to meet Jesus, the Holy Spirit, and ultimately, I began to draw close to God.

Somewhere in all this, I realized that God had been waiting for me. He was waiting for me to come to Him, to talk to Him, and give Him my heart. That was the first time in my life I felt truly wanted and special. God is a gentleman and won't force Himself on us. We must want to accept God on His terms. We must confess our sins and ask Jesus to be our Savior. For a good portion of my life, I lived in emotional pain and upheaval. I spent years in and out of counseling. Now I can function without day-in-and-day-out counseling, and when I hit a snag in life's journey, I find a few sessions with my minister will get me back on my feet.

JOHN

The Word Became Flesh

1 In the beginning was the Word, and the Word was with God, and the Word was God. ²He was with God in the beginning.

³Through him all things were made; without him nothing was made that has been made. ⁴In him was life, and that life was the light of men. ⁵The light shines in the darkness, but the darkness has not understood it.

⁶There came a man who was sent from God; his name was John. ⁷He came as a witness to testify concerning that light, so that through him all men might believe. ⁸He himself was not the light; he came only as a witness to the light. ⁹The true light that gives light to every man was coming into the world.

¹⁰He was in the world, and though the world was made through him, the world did not recognize him. ¹¹He came to that which was his own, but his own did not receive him. ¹²Yet to all who received him, to those who believed in his name, he gave the right to become children of God— ¹³children born not of natural descent, nor of human decision or a husband's will, but born of God.

¹⁴The Word became flesh and made his dwelling among us. We have seen his glory, the glory of the One and Only, who came from the Father, full of grace and truth.

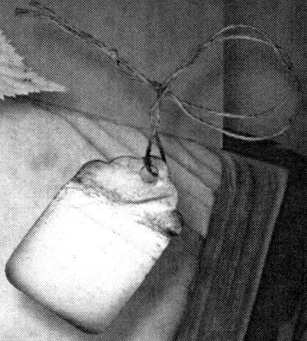

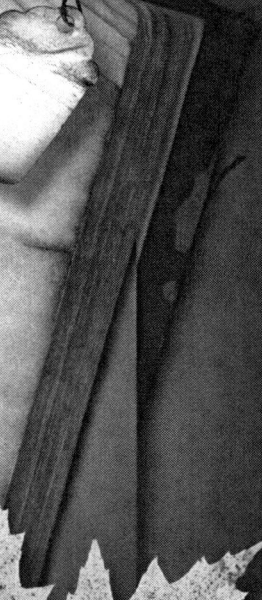

¹⁵John testifies concerning him. He cries out, saying, "This was he of whom I said, 'He who comes after me has surpassed me because he was before me.'" ¹⁶From the fullness of his grace we have all received one blessing after another.

CHAPTER 1

ACCOLADES

As I began my faith journey, I learned it was important to tell God how wonderful He is. I remember wondering, Why do I need to tell God He is wonderful? He should know, He is the creator. Why does God need me to tell Him what He already knows? I was full of doubts and questions.

As my faith developed, I learned to "just do it," that understanding may come later, and also that sometimes, I won't understand.

As I began telling God how wonderful He is, I began to appreciate Him, to love Him, and most importantly, I began to place God at the center of my heart. As I started to place Him at the center of my heart, I found myself desiring to change my character. I found myself wanting to please God. It was like when I was a little girl and I wanted to please my parents. I learned what they did not like and tried to stay away from those things.

I did not have proper respect for my earthly father. He was a hard man. His anger was ever present. My earthly father came from an abusive home. He had polio at twenty-three with a wife and three small children in his care. My father's anger was a constant in our home. I did not trust men. To be honest, it took me a very long time to trust that God really loved me.

I often tell people that I came to my faith through the back door. I grew up with a dad who had many struggles of his own and was not always the greatest male role model. I did not choose well for my first husband. My second husband has taught me many things. He has shown me the face of Jesus through his gentle care of me. And my husband can be tough when he needs to; but with me, he has always been gentle, compassionate, and kind. My husband showed me the face of Jesus; and with that, I have been able to trust God, that Jesus truly loves me. I came to my faith through the back door. I was able to learn that God is tender and caring. In that tender love, I began a faith journey that is wonderful.

As the years have passed, I find telling God every day—and sometimes throughout the day—how wonderful He is. He has been a blessing.

In our human relationships, we tend to have people we look up to. We want to please them, to be at their side a whole lot. As I go through my faith journey, I have a desire to be near God, to draw close to Him, and to please Him.

I have also learned that men and women come to God in different ways. Men are not all about feelings like women generally are. As a woman, I tend to seek the tender parts of God. Through the years when I have struggled, God has given me gentleness. When I first was coming to the Lord, I was going through a painful struggle in my life. My heart was breaking. I was riding an exercise bike, reading my Bible, and praying. I started to cry. In my spirit, I felt God telling me to look up. It was like He was telling me to look into His eyes, and I felt His hand on my chin. More recently, I was again going through a struggle. We had moved to Virginia, and our home has a large porch. I found myself sitting on it day after day. I would do my Bible study and sit and look out at the nature around me. As I sat there, I saw hummingbirds fly to the feeder and saw deer. A rabbit would hop by, and a mother cat fed her babies. Day after day, I found healing and peace when I sat out there. It felt like God was hugging me.

Men generally don't crave tenderness like women do. Men operate on respect. They need to respect each other and feel respected. One gentleman said he sees God in the foxhole next to him. Another said that he struggles with submission. Men see themselves as the leader, defender, and it is a struggle to submit to God.

One of the stories that I have heard men relate to is Jesus throwing the money changers out of the temple. It is scary to me as a woman. A man will see it as Jesus took a stand even if it wasn't **a** popular **one**. He was willing to do what needed to be done.

As I move along in my accolades, I find myself thanking God for His Son, Jesus, and then I thank Jesus for coming into our world. To be honest, it took me a very long time to comprehend the need for Jesus. I was of the camp that thought we were basically good but misunderstood.

In the beginning of my faith journey, I remember being repulsed at the cross. The horror I felt when I learned that our Savior was literally nailed to the cross made me sick to my stomach. I felt that it was barbaric. Why would a loving God allow His son to die that type of death? I also felt that if your actions did not hurt others—such as drinking, doing drugs, and having sex as long as it was consensual—what was the problem?

As I have gone on in life, I found that what we do does affect everyone around us. Drinking and drugs affect the family. How many kids have had a parent not show up to an important event? It shows up in the workplace as well. How many employers deal with high employee absenteeism? In my own family, we have at least three generations where abuse has been the norm. My grandfather and grandmother were both very abusive. My grandfather, in a fit of anger, plunged a pitchfork into my uncle's foot. The week he died at seventy-some years old, he was chasing Grandma around trying to beat her with a broomstick. My dad often beat us kids till we were black and blue. In my first marriage, there was abuse as well. As far as I can tell, the abuse has finally left the family line. I do not know of it going on in my children's families.

Sexual unfaithfulness also impacts more than just the couple engaging in the sex. It breaks up families. Sexually transmitted diseases abound. We were created to be one man and one woman. The more sex partners you have, the higher chance of acquiring sexually transmitted diseases. Women who engage in many sex partners also have a higher chance for cervical cancer. The list goes on.

From my twenties through my early forties, I found myself in and out of counseling. I had deep emotional pain and did not know how to cope. As I went through a divorce after twenty-four years of marriage, I began to meet Jesus. I had been in church from childhood, still I had extreme emotional pain and, for some reason, did not understand meeting Jesus on a personal level. As I lay in bed after my divorce, I started a prayer very awkwardly, but I prayed. I asked God to allow me to be in a relationship again, and this time, I wanted to be in a healthy relationship. I asked God to bring me to that relationship when I was ready. I asked for a man who took his faith seriously. I was not interested in great wealth. I just wanted to be able to meet our financial obligations. I wanted to look up to my husband, to be able to listen to his direction, and to be able to respect him. I prayed for this a few times and then I went on with my life. I went to work, I volunteered at church, and I helped get my mother's house in shape for her retirement. I continued in counseling that I had started with my ex-husband. I went to a divorce recovery class and met some new friends. One day, I met my husband. I wanted to practice dating. We wound up dating and then marrying. We hit it off right from the start and felt very comfortable with each other. I believe God brought us together. Our marriage is a very comfortable marriage. I believe God is the center of our marriage and that is why we are so content.

My counselor was a Christian. He was a retired minister. He was old enough to be my father, grandfather even. I began to form a bond with this man. I trusted him. I felt safe with him. He began to open my eyes to make Jesus my best friend. This was a new concept to me. As he counseled me, he gave me a prayer format. It is ACTSS. I took this concept home and began to pray it through.

My life for the most part was filled with emotional pain, and I struggled to get through life day by day. When my marriage ended after twenty-four years, I found myself at my lowest point. It is then I began my faith journey in earnest.

I am not a fan of the name-it-and-claim-it theology. God does want us to come to Him with our requests. As I have come along in my faith journey, I believe that when I ask for things I need to ask for the things in God's heart. I learn what's in God's heart by reading the Bible and by praying. He will reveal to us His heart if we show an interest in learning *who* God is.

As I learned to begin talking to Jesus, I began to know Him. I found God pointing at me to look at the cross. I did not want to; it was a horrible death. I had, through the years, "softened" the cross, thinking it wasn't that bad. As I began to submit and look, my eyes were opened. In the horribleness of the cross, I began to see how *ugly* sin was to God. Even the little sins were an abomination to God. To God, any sin is the same, so my white lies were on the same par as murder.

Let me walk through a few of the things our Lord endured for us. After the Last Supper, Jesus went to the garden to pray. He was troubled, deeply troubled. He began to sweat drops of blood as he agonized about what He was going to face. This type of medical problem has been reported on in medical journals. It does happen. After the soldiers came to take Jesus away, His disciples left Him. Next, our Lord was scourged, that meant he was whipped. The whips had bone fragments and bits of glass tied to the ends of the whip. This tore into His flesh and possibly even some of His backbone might have shown through at the end of the whipping. Next, He was mocked. Mocking wasn't just calling Him names, they beat Him as well. His face was disfigured, swollen, bruised, and maybe even other parts were bruised as well. To add insult to injury, a crown of thorns was forcefully placed on his head. After all that, He was expected to carry His cross. He was weak, and another man was forced to carry it for Him. On the hill, the Lord Jesus was nailed to the cross. He literally had nails pounded into His flesh. I marvel at what He endured and that He was able to minister even after all that pain. On the cross, our Lord Jesus asked God to forgive us, for we did not know what we were doing. Next, He gave His mother Mary to John. Finally, He ministered to the thief on the cross next to Him. Our Savior died. Many times in my prayers, I want to cry, to stop looking; and God encourages me to move along. Next, I see that Jesus has risen, and that is the wonderful gift we have been given—our Lord rising from the dead. At this point, my heart is filled with joy. Lately, I marvel anew at our Savior. When He came back to be with his disciples for forty days, He came back with love, not bitterness. Our Lord did not fuss at His disciples for leaving Him at the cross. He came back with love, patience, and further instructed them so they could "go forth and make disciples of every nation and tribe."

One last thought, Jesus was hung on the cross naked. I cannot imagine the embarrassment our Lord felt. Then I think, God loved us that much to be naked for us. God's love is that open for us, to us.

At this point, I find myself thanking Jesus over and over. He has given me a hope and a future. My hope is now. Many days, my hope helps me get up and face the day. It helps me stay the course when I'd rather give up. My hope is also about my future. The Bible teaches me that if I accept Jesus as my Savior, allow Him to enter my heart, that means I am allowing Him to change me; then my future is eternity in heaven and not in hell. Through the years, I've learned that I need to make room for Jesus. He does not want to reside in a lot of junk.

God is faithful. He will help you through your struggles. He will help you clean the house so to speak so that He and Jesus can reside there all the time. When I came to the Lord, I had a lot of anger, bitterness, pornographic thoughts, and a heavy dose of hurt. As I prayed, God revealed to me the junk I had in my life. As He revealed to me this junk, He also provided ways for me to rid myself of it. God speaks to me through my heart (conscience). Most of my junk appeared in my morning shower. I would allow myself to let my mind go where it willed. It usually focused on the hurt, the anger, the pornographic thoughts; and I'd come out of the shower a very unhappy woman. I found myself desiring to sing in the shower—not me really. As I learned to sing hymns and praise songs, I even had to memorize them, I found myself getting out of the shower a lot happier.

I also would pray and ask God to help me with something and then find myself dwelling on it. I call this "helping God help me." I wasn't able to move off a hurt or struggle. God reminded me of a retreat I had gone on where a wooden cross was placed in the center of the group. People came forward and nailed their problem to the cross. I asked my husband to make me a large wooden cross, had it hung up in our basement, and when I had a problem, I nailed my struggle to that cross. Then when I tried to help God with the struggle, God would remind me that the struggle was nailed to the cross. I soon found myself leaving the struggle on the cross and my spirit and my emotional well-being was calmer. There are many ways to let go of pain. I have friends who place an empty box on their dresser and they write their problem on a piece of paper and put in the box.

Part of my accolades is to thank the Holy Spirit. I needed to learn how to talk to the Holy Spirit. I could never figure out who the Holy Spirit was. I never understood Him. By speaking to Him, I've come to know Him. In meeting Him, I begin to understand the Trinity and His role in it.

The Holy Spirit is my helper. He teaches me and guides me. In the process of learning, I find my relationship with God the Father, God the Son, and God the Holy Spirit growing deeper. The deeper my walk, the more confidence I have to live life and to face life. I generally find myself thanking the Holy Spirit. Then after that, I request that He teach me. My prayer goes something like, "Teach me Holy Spirit, the love, the will, the desire of the Father and weave it into the fabric of my being so that every fiber is of the Father and for His glory. Teach me to love, to serve and to give love, and bring and lay love at the Father's feet so that He would get the glory." In this, I find myself learning how to love a lot deeper; I am able to give God the recognition, and I find that I don't need to be the *center* of all this. It is learning how to agape love, seek another's highest good. Agape love is a wonderful gift to learn. Anyone who knows me knows I used to make everything about me. Agape love teaches me to reach out to others, to meet them where they are at, and to love them there. As God has loved me right where I was at, I have been able to overcome and love as I am loved.

This part of my prayer tends to be the longest. I believe it is a very important process in the prayer though. First, I get to know God on a more personal level. As God opens my eyes and heart, I find so much healing over all in my life. I find a desire to know God on a deep level. I also find that by the time I get to my requests, the process helps me to put things in a right perspective.

When I was three years old, I climbed up on the bathroom sink, opened the medicine cabinet, and found a bottle of aspirin. I opened the bottle and ate a whole lot of the aspirins. When my mother found me, I remember saying that I "ate candy." My mother called the police, and I was rushed to the hospital. I remember bits and pieces of that day. I remember being on a bed. I remember bright lights. I remember I felt a wonderful sense of peace and love, and all of a sudden, my eyes were open and I was angry. I've had people through the years dismiss my feelings. I felt that I died and I was with God the Father feeling that perfect love. I was angry when I woke up because that wonderful sense of perfect love was gone.

Many days, I feel the closeness I felt back then with the Father. This time, I don't get angry when that closeness is not there. I feel a peace deep inside of me that God is near me. I feel safe enough now to move about life. Somewhere down deep inside me, I know that God is near. It is kind of like when I learned how to ride a bike. I was terrified when my Dad took his hand off the seat and allowed me to ride by myself. When I learned that his hand was off and I had ridden a long way, I was so proud of myself. That is how I feel now with God the Father; when His hand is off me, I sense He is allowing me to "ride" on my own. Of course, my "ride" longs to be in line with God the Father and His holy ways. I don't want to go off in my own direction. I want to go off in God's direction. That then gives me a wonderful sense of accomplishment.

The Trinity of God the Father, God the Son, and God the Holy Spirit is a very difficult concept to grasp and understand. For me, speaking to each one helps me to understand, to respect God, and to begin to fully grasp God and His perfect design in all things. As I go through this prayer process, I find that my prayer requests begin to align with God and His heart and that my desires then become more of what God wants us to be—to request not all about me and my selfishness.

Chapter 2

Confession

I have often heard that "confession is good for the soul." The more I journey along with Jesus, the more I believe that statement is true. For a good portion of my life, I thought that God did not understand. I felt that we each had our own deep hurts and wondered how we could ever meet God's stringent requirements. I felt that God doesn't understand how hard it is to forgive, to get past all the hurts in life. I truly did not get that God understood and provided a way for each of us to overcome, hurt, sin, and all the ugliness of life.

I could not grasp why we needed to confess. I could not get why we are sinners and that we needed to ask God to forgive us. It did not make sense to me. God should know how I felt.

As I learned to pray this prayer though, I began to see differently. I often hear throughout the scriptures, "Eyes that see and ears that hear." This thought comes back to me over and over for many of life's strange ways. The more I open my heart to Jesus, the more I begin to understand that God's ways may seem strange; but when I do them, life then begins to not hurt, and it even makes sense to me.

I felt beat up by life without examining my every flaw. It hurt to think that I could not do anything right. At one point though, I began asking God to forgive me. At first, I only asked to be forgiven. I then learned that I need to be specific. Now when I ask God to forgive me, I tend to go through a list to start with, it is common everyday stuff for me; and at this point, I don't want to go back to these struggles.

My list generally starts out like, "Lord God, please forgive me for my sins. Help me to walk away from pride, arrogance, intolerance, impatience, lust, greed, envy, bitterness, jealousy, anger, unforgivingness, fear, and anxiety."

When I looked at my life, these were the common struggles I dealt with. I grew up in an angry home. Violence was used on us kids. As the oldest, I tended to be violent with my siblings. Violence seemed to be the way to handle life. If someone would not do what you wanted, then you needed to slug them. That made sense to me.

Along with all the anger, I also found a lot of impatience, intolerance, and even some arrogance and bitterness thrown into this mix. For me, fear and anxiety were natural consequences to this lifestyle. As life went on, lust, greed, envy, and the rest of the struggles seemed to play heavily into my life.

By the time I gave my heart to Jesus, I was a wounded, hurting woman. I had spent years in and out of counseling. I would go for a while and stop, only to find out that I was hurting again. I wound up being in an abusive marriage, and I could not find any peace. Peace is something I longed for and I could not find, even with counseling.

My last counselor was a Christian. He kept pointing me to Jesus. He taught me how to handle my hurt, which by that time turned into anger inside. I struggled to let go of those violent ways. I refused to spank my children, I did very rarely, and then I felt bad when I got angry. I had never seen spankings done with love. Later in life, I learned with James Dobson's *Dare to Discipline* how to spank with love. I had only seen them done with anger. I did not want to give into that anger all the time. I had a tendency to stuff my anger and then I would blow up, throw things, scream, and was still out of control.

As I began to get specific with my sins, asking God to forgive me, I found myself walking away from depression, anger, hurt, and a whole lot of these struggles—sins. I found that God was giving me what counseling did not. God gave me courage to look at my flaws, my hurt, etc., then He gave me the tools to truly let go and to leave behind these struggles. For the first time in my life, I began to have peace. I was starting to look outside of myself and what was being done to me.

As I let go of these struggles, sin, I began to see that I also struggled with some people in my life. Some did not like me—I want everyone to like me, and I am in great pain when people don't. I also had some people in my life I could not understand no matter how hard I tried. Some were repulsive to me. If we are to be honest, there are always people in our lives we need to have more grace and charity toward.

I then started asking God to help me love those people in my life that I found unlovable. This too has been healing. God tells us that we need to forgive if we want to be forgiven. I remember God telling me to love someone who did not like me, has done some mean things to me, etc. I cried and asked God why. God just said, "Love that person." I did not even know how to love that person; I did not like that person a whole lot. So I had to ask God to show me how. He was faithful and begun to show me. I can say that I love this person now.

Sometimes, I also find that God wants my attitude to be right. I may not be in a day-to-day relationship with this person, but my attitude needs to be a loving one though. When I married my current husband, he insisted I pray for my ex-husband. Again, I did not want to—I had a lot of hurt and anger toward him. I did start praying for him though. I now don't harbor any bitterness toward him. I truly don't want harm to come to him. Do I want to be his best friend? No! Still, I don't harbor any bitterness toward him either. I can pray for his well-being now and mean it.

As life plays itself out, I also find moments where I gossip, have x-rated thoughts, get out to the car and see an item that I did not pay for in the buggy—stuff that is wrong. I now attempt to make things right, like take the item back into the store and pay for it. I find days when my mind is going along on a track I don't like, so now I pray, "Lord, take this thought from me." God is faithful. I am amazed that a thought disappears after I pray that.

Lastly, I try to ask God to forgive me for sins I am unaware of. There are always things we do that aren't good, yet we don't know we do them. I will often ask God to bring to light these sins and then I ask that He would forgive me and show me how to walk away from them. Once more, I find God being faithful. He will show me and then provide a way to walk away from those sins.

Will we ever be perfect? Adam and Eve were the ones who entered into sin, and now, each of us are born into sin. I am finally able to accept that I cannot and will not ever be perfect now. This brings peace to my soul. When I "hear" Satan's accusations though, I am able to say, "Away with you." I know that Jesus died for me. I accept that gift now. As I accept that Jesus died for me, I find a desire born in me to tell about the wonderful gift of salvation and redemption.

Another prayer I often pray is, "Lord Jesus, you are the light in my heart and the hope in my soul. I see that broken down to look like a flashlight shining into my heart. I see the light landing on a corner in my heart and Jesus is saying, "There, you need to look at that." Then I see God helping me to overcome that obstacle. Next, I see hope. For me, hope has two sides. I first see hope in this life. I am able to face the trials of life now. I can accept easier the fact that I may not be liked or wanted. When I am hurting deeply, I find God coming alongside of me. He comforts me and that may mean sitting on my porch and watching nature happen, rabbits hopping by, a crane standing along the river bank, or a hummingbird coming in for a drink. As I accept these gifts of love, I find then that I have a future hope too. That future hope is heaven. Only recently have I fully grasped that there is hell. Hell is a scary place, and it will be for eternity. The Bible talks about hell, and again, it is scary.

Lastly I pray, "Lord, you are my bread of life and my cup of salvation." With this, I am telling Jesus that He is my all. He is my sustenance. I have come to realize that I am nothing without Jesus's wonderful gift of the cross. As I take communion, I find a deep peace—I am once more remembering until Jesus comes back with the gift I have been given in His death on the cross.

CHAPTER 3

THANKFUL

Being thankful is a huge blessing to learn. I first learned to admit I was a sinner and found peace. Next, I learned to be thankful.

As I learn to be thankful, I find that I see what I do have, and I don't focus so much on what I don't have. I learn to be content with what I have as well.

For me lately, I find that stuff can own me, and I am trapped by my stuff. I have an aunt who had so much stuff. She owned a three-story house. She could not shut the front door due to stuff. She was moving to another floor because her stuff had overrun her first floor and was even crowding out her second floor.

God keeps teaching me that He will supply what I need. I am learning the difference between what I want and what I need. As I think on this, I am learning to start seeing what I really need. I need food to eat, but I don't need junk food. I need water to drink. I need a roof over my head. I need love. I need to feel valued as a human being. I need clothes to wear, but I don't need the latest style—only basic clothes. I need a way to clean my body, teeth, etc. I need a safe place to sleep. I need a way to get to work. When I break down what I need, I begin to appreciate what I do have. Much of what I do have is beyond what I need.

As a child, money was hard to come by for my parents. My dad had polio. Women did not generally work back then. Mom had to go to work so we could have a place to live, to eat, etc. Right after Dad had polio, people came to our rescue. We had moved in with our grandma. She worked. She was a widow raising a son. She worked in a cafeteria. Her work often sent food home to us. Our church family also helped provide for us.

As they were able, Mom went to work. When Dad got a little better, he got a job. Dad could not do construction work anymore, but he did what he was capable of. Mom eventually went to college. That allowed her to earn more money. My parents were grateful for the work and the opportunity to support their family. They did not stay in the "system" of help. They helped themselves. God provided for them. First it was Grandma, the church, and then it was a job.

Growing up at home was hard. Dad was angry. Mom was busy working. I feel that the main goal was to make sure there was a roof over our heads and food on the table. There was little extra energy for the nurturing we needed. So how can I be thankful? I am very thankful to be honest. I am thankful to Grandma for taking us in. I am thankful to the church. I am thankful for Grandma's work sending food home. I am thankful even for the craziness of our life. In all that craziness, I learned how to be a good worker. I learned loyalty. I learned how to stick out hard times. I learned how to roll with the punches. I am very thankful for our neighbors. One couple came by to check on us, to bring us fruits. When my parents weren't around, this couple would settle our fights—help us with kid emergencies.

The older I get, the more I find myself thankful for the struggles I have or have had in life. These struggles will allow me to meet people who have needs that I am familiar with. I know the pain of abuse. My abused past allows me to reach out and offer hope. Hope is what gets me up in the morning and out the door. When I live my life, people are watching me. I have a coworker who watched me after my divorce. She knew my story. She watched me as I struggled with being single after twenty-four years of marriage. As I was retiring, she e-mailed me with her struggle—abuse that was going on in her life. I was able to meet her where she was at and then we went to a recovery group together. She has begun her journey with the Lord, and she will someday reach a troubled person and give them her hand.

After I retired, I started water aerobics. Some days, I swam laps after the class. One day, a lady and I were talking. I was telling her of my past and the struggles I had. I tend to talk about my past not to get sympathy, but in the hopes of reaching out a hand to someone who may need encouragement and realize they do not have to put up with abuse, etc. As we talked, I stated that I was against abortion. This lady suggested that I should have been aborted because of my troubled life.

Through the years, I learned that God tends to use us as His hands. I am starting to believe that is why as a Christian I have a great desire to reach out to people. All the pain that I had of being abused, of feeling unwanted, or of being rejected allows me to reach outside of myself and reach toward another person. I am learning a new way of living my life. I learned in Sunday school about agape love. Agape love is seeking another person's highest good. When I am seeking another person's highest good, I am not all into me and my problems.

Many years ago, I was a high school youth advisor. My marriage was rocky. I had two children. When I was with the teens, I found a few hours each week where my struggles were not in the front of my mind. I was able to reach out to these teens.

When I look at God, I tend to see that He uses agape love with us. He is always seeking our highest good. If we give our hearts to Jesus and ask

Him to be our Savior, then one day we will live in heaven. If I understand correctly, what we learn here on earth will be used in heaven.

After Adam and Eve sinned, they were kicked out of the garden. God did not just throw them to the wolves, so to speak. He killed an animal and then made clothes for them to wear. Later, God sent His only Son to reconcile us to Him.

God provided for my family. God was there after my divorce as well. I learned to pray at that point, and I started to ask Jesus as my Savior soon afterward. That is the point where I began a genuine faith journey.

Until I met Jesus as my Savior, truly began to talk to Him, to trust Him, I felt unwanted, not strong, and had absolutely no hope. As I have learned to love Jesus/God, I find each day to be a blessing. I am grateful for all aspects of my life. I have gone through a lot of feelings of rejection from people close to me. I have cried to God, and He has given me a hope and a future. At one point in my life, I would have "wrapped" my house around me and tried not to go outside. Now though, I am able to walk out the front door and face each day. Sometimes, life hurts still. With Jesus though, I find I can "let go and let God."

For me, being thankful has taught me much. I have more than I need. I have people in my life who do love me, even if I am annoying. I do not need year-in-and-year-out counseling like I once did. When I do hurt, God allows me to cry to Him. He doesn't get tired of me talking about my problems too much.

I would like to end this chapter with a challenge. Each day, list five things you are thankful for. I did this after my divorce. At first, it was hard. The more I did it though, the sweeter I found life.

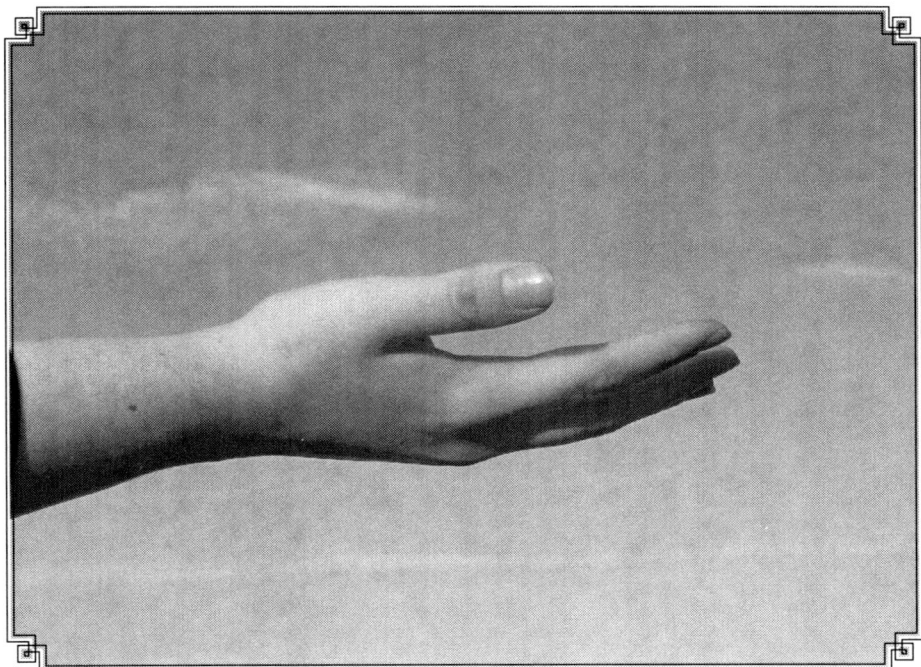

Chapter 4

SUPPLICATIONS

I have had an idea of what supplication is through the years. As I began to write, I thought I would look it up in the dictionary just to be sure. As per Webster's Collegiate Dictionary, fifth edition *Supplication* means "entreating; asking submissively and a humble petition, solicitation."

I have not been too far off in my thoughts, which makes me feel good. For me at this point in the prayer, I begin to ask from God. As I have read the Bible and studied it, I believe that God wants to give to us. I also don't believe that God is a magical being who grants us every tiny request just to shower us with gifts for the sake of gifts just to buy our love. I do believe God likes to give to us though. I also believe if we want then we need to learn who God is and what God likes. The more I read my Bible, the more I learn what is important to Him. He often says to the Israelites (paraphrased), "Love justice, hate evil, help the widow and the orphan, use proper weights and measures."

When I am hurting, God comforts me. I can ask for comfort when I feel beat up by life. God has done that so wonderfully through the years. Lately as I pray through our Lord's final hours, I am focused on Jesus in the garden. He leaves the disciples and goes to pray. He prays for the cup of suffering to be taken from him. I am a wimp. I am not good with pain, and I have panicked through the years as I wondered how I would deal with physical torture for His sake.

It happens all the time all around the world. In some countries, a person cannot change from that country's religion to Christianity. If they do, then the new Christian is persecuted. It is not pretty what is done to them. They are tortured, their family will disown them, and they even may be killed. So I have been scared as to how I would handle myself for the Gospel. One day as I was praying through this piece, I realized that our Lord was scared. My husband said the pain is not what scared Him as much as being separated from the Father. For me, I also felt that fear of facing all that abuse. I focus on the pain. He suffered greatly with a pain that I can't even imagine.

As often happens when I pray, I heard God say, "Go on." Our Lord prayed this prayer three times. At one point, he started sweating drops of blood. To me, that is fear. Father God said "go on" again to me. The third time our Lord prayed this, our Father sent angels to comfort Him. Our Lord loved us enough to go through and not back out of all that abuse, pain, and separation. I see the angels comforting Him. That helps me face struggles. I may not get angels each time, but I find comfort. I have found comfort in my cat snuggling me when I hurt. I have found comfort in my husband's arms. I have been comforted out there on my front porch as I watch nature pass me by and listened to the sound of the river behind our house. I have even found comfort on the phone.

Recently, I was re-entering someone's life I had not seen in years. We had struggled, and finally, I quit seeing that person. As I was re-entering this person's life, I also realized that they saw me as they had years ago. I was allowing myself to be that person again. The phone calls went out to girlfriends who, as I talked, began to reflect back to me the Janet of today, the Janet who had become a new creation in Christ. I had been praying to love this person. Father God has given me a prayer to pray when people are hard for me to love. I pray, "Lord teach me to love those I find unlovable."

I mention them by name, maybe even the struggle. God again has been faithful. He has taught me to love those I struggle to love.

At this point, I find myself looking at our Lord on the cross. His back is nothing but raw flesh, torn and bleeding and full of pain. His head hurts because of the thorns dug into it, and his face is swollen due to being beaten. Finally, I see the nails pounded into His flesh. Pain! Oh my, the pain! Our Lord up on that cross in all that pain. He prays up there, "Father, forgive them, for they know not what they are doing." I don't know how much time passes, but next, He gives His mother Mary to John to live with him. She was then cared for till her death. Lastly, he tells the thief that He will be in paradise. That is three times our Lord ministers in all that pain! Wow! Our Lord endured through all that. Again, I realize that the angels brought Him comfort.

At this point, I begin to have a heart for people. I pray for them, for their struggles. I also know God knows what is best for them, so I pray for His will in their lives. I remember a close family member who was going through a rough time. He would call me early in the morning or even late at night. He would apologize for calling at such an hour. I remember telling him that was okay. I remember telling him that I was able to go to sleep because I had placed him in God's hands. To me, that was the best place for this person to be—in God's hands. I felt comforted and was able to sleep because no one could care for him like God could.

I pray for each family member. I pray for neighbors, past and present. I pray for friends. I pray for old coworkers. (I am now retired, but I have not forgotten old friends.) I even pray for my ex and his family. I pray for people who are sick or struggling. I pray for the girls in my "survivors of abuse" group. I end up praying for missionaries and for radio stations because that is what I listen to a lot. I pray for people who are serving the Lord. If I've been asked to pray for people, then I also will lift them up as well.

I also ask God to help me be what He wants me to be. At this point in my life, I don't want to be not with the Father. I have felt a love I had never known. Father God trusts me and gives me work to do, and I love that. Each day, I ask God to help me be the writer He is creating me to be. I ask to write His words and not mine. Father God uses my life as a witness. That is what I want, to share how He has worked in my life. I may also ask for Father God to help me have the right heart.

At this point, I begin to have a desire to serve.

CHAPTER 5

SERVICE

I have a strong desire to serve. In my heart, I believe that as a Christian, our hearts have a tendency to want to reach out and touch others. I feel that is our desire because our God reaches out and touches us, and we want to give back. I also am not a "works" fan. Some people tend to do "good" works just to receive from God. I believe my heart needs to be in the right place as I offer to do for others. I also believe that God looks at our heart, not just the outward expressions of our lives. He looks past the layers of our lives to the core of who we are and why we choose to do what we do.

Many years ago, I was a youth advisor at the church I belonged to at the time. That was my first long-term commitment in giving back to the Lord. As I look back on those years, I believe that I was given as much as I gave.

The men in my life were hard men. They were a struggle for me to deal with. I felt that men did not really have feelings. The young men in those years taught me so much. For the first time, I got it. I saw them struggle with relationships, trying to make the young lady happy, being upset when the relationship went sour, and even, at times, trying to get up the nerve to ask a girl out. I finally saw young men have feelings, and it was so precious.

We often took the kids on retreats and work camps. Those retreats allowed my "mom mode" to really kick in. Many nights, I asked the girls if they needed me to tuck them in. I'd sit on the corner of the bed talking to them for a minute and then ask if they wanted a hug. At that point, if they wanted one, I gave them one. Many times, I was nurse as well. If the kids got sick, I was the one to hover over them. One time, a young man had a seizure and was admitted to the hospital. I sat with him the next day while the rest of the group was out working. There was also the young lady who vomited all over everything and could not stop. We had to take her to the hospital. I went along and babied her while she got looked at by the doctors. I often was a cook at the retreats and work camps as well. Kids were assigned to help me in the kitchen. I had many wonderful moments there as well. There is something about chopping vegetables and talking. Kids would share dreams, fears, and life in general as we chopped, sautéed, and worked in the kitchen.

I started to feel I had value as I gave my heart to these kids. Up to that point, I never felt I had value. Did I know it at the time? No. It is something I see on hindsight. I remember always trying to get noticed. I tried to draw attention to myself. I wanted to be somebody. I wanted to be loved, wanted, and thought highly of. Those teens accepted me as I had never been accepted. It felt wonderful.

As I began life with my current husband, we both have had a need to reach out. When we were first married, we volunteered to help put on workshops for the remarried. I learned a whole new set of skills doing that. I learned how to call and set up speakers for each week. We have gone on short-term mission trips through the years. At one point, I was being taught by God that giving doesn't only involve being in an organized church setting. I did not feel I was truly giving unless it was in an organized setting.

At that point, God started teaching me to give outside the church. As my faith grew, I started to want to give at work. I loved to walk in the parking garage at work. It had inclines, which helped build my thighs. Many days as I was going back into work, others were coming into the garage to leave. I found myself opening the door and holding it for them. We had to swipe our pass through a device to get in the garage. This saved them from swiping the badge and many times looking for their badge. I was learning the little unnoticed ways to serve God. If someone did not have enough money to buy something in line and I had it, sometimes I'd pay the difference for that person. Sometimes, I would bring back a beverage when I went to the cafeteria for a coworker.

Prior to our leaving Michigan, a lady stopped by as we sat on the porch one day. She had applied for a position at the group home next door. She asked for a ride home, about an hour from us. My husband and I took her home. She was needy. We gave her some furniture, old dishes, etc.

Down here in Virginia, I continue to learn how to give outside the church. My landlord is a sickly lady. Getting out of the house is difficult many days. She has emphysema, and it takes a toll on her. I find great joy in visiting her. She is old enough to be my mother, so I have fun talking with her. My own mother has been gone now for many years.

I also believe it is important to give some of my money. My husband and I try very hard to give to the church we belong to. We also find many other organizations in which we have a desire to give to. I think it is important to put our money where our hearts are. I believe this is a service to the Lord as well.

We automatically try to tithe to the church. We feel that God has asked us to give a tithe as we read our Bible, so we try to do that. We also feel that it is important to give extra, and we have found that God honors us. I believe that if we desire to give and are willing to give, then God will also provide for us to have enough to give. God says, "Test me." We have tested God, and He has always given us enough so that we can give.

Many women in the church love to bring a dish of food to someone who is sick, to someone in the hospital, or to someone grieving. Me, I'm not good at that. There are also the ones who will send out cards to the sick. Again, I'm not good at this type of service. I am not the one to help with mailings either. They are worthwhile ways to give, but for me though, it doesn't work.

I go to prayer often asking God to show me what He wants me to do or to give. I have had to study what my talents are. I have a talent for writing—not note cards, but writing my thoughts, my feelings. Through the years, God has helped me to write. First, my friend J got with me for a couple of years and helped me to learn to write. I also have written a note to my husband almost every day—it is a ministry, and it helps me with my writing as well. In my first marriage, I found myself losing respect for my husband. I now write to my husband and tell him each day his good qualities. If I am telling him what I like, I find it hard to lose respect for him. My friend S and I wrote a newsletter for the remarried group at church. I learned how to interview couples and write about them. God has helped me to become a writer. He has placed people in my path and then He has given me opportunities to write. As I grow in my writing, then I look for new writing projects. I have written a blog now for a couple of years, and at this point, I am writing my first book. I believe God is helping me to write and is giving me writing projects. I also believe God is a God of action, not inaction. I need to seek, and then I need to do. I tend to sense God's calling and then I need to go forth and do. Many people fear that God will call them to serve in a foreign country that has no modern equipment. I believe if you are called to that, you for the most part will have a desire to do it.

At this point, I am at a new church. I am learning the church, and I hope to one day find the niche where I can volunteer my time. For now though, I wait, I grow, and I learn. I also continue to look for ways to serve, to give those who are not in the church but are part of my everyday life. Again, prayer and Bible study helps me to see opportunities to serve and to give. Prayer and Bible study helps me by opening my heart to God and then searching for ways to please Him.

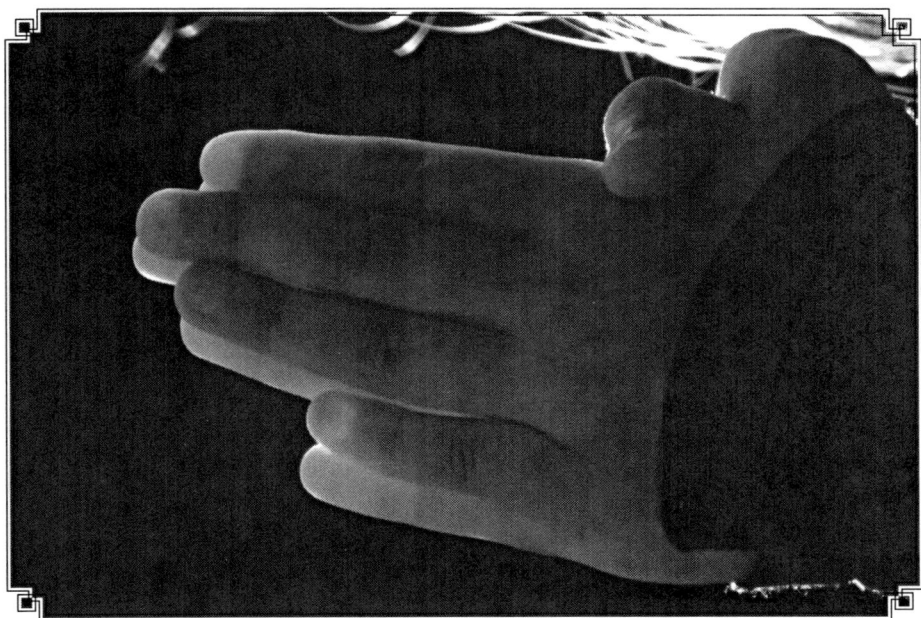

CHAPTER 6

ACTSS: THE PRAYER

Below is a sample of my prayer; it does change from day to day and situation to situation. Sometimes when I am in extreme pain, I may only tell God that I am hurting. Still, it is this format that has brought me to a wholeness I had never known before.

"Father God, Abba, oh Lord God, you are holy. You are righteous, faithful, and steadfast. You are the most high God, the only true God. You are the rock I grasp on to. You are the only true God. I love you, I worship you, and I adore you. I praise you. You are the God of Abraham, Isaac, and Jacob. You give me/us grace, mercy, and compassion. I praise you, I worship you, and I adore you. You are the God of creation. You have created the plants that feed us. You give us wool, cotton, and leather to clothe our bodies with. You give us fruits and vegetables. You created the mountains, the rivers, and the oceans. What a mighty God you are.

"Lord, you sent your only Son; whoever believes in Him shall not perish but have everlasting life. Lord Jesus, you came to us. You walked among the worst of us. You loved us, gave us hope. You showed us our God. You are my teacher, my friend, my intercessor. Lord Jesus, you are the light in my heart. You are the hope in my soul. You are my bread of life and the cup of my salvation. In you, Lord Jesus, I have hope for today and tomorrow, that hope helps me walk out the front door each day, Lord Jesus. Thank you, Lord Jesus. I come to your cross again today, Lord Jesus. You endured the cross for me, for all who will believe. Thank you. Thank you for all you went through. First, you were scourged. Lord Jesus, they whipped you, tore the flesh off your back even the bones of your backbone were bare. You were mocked. Lord Jesus, that was mean too. You were beaten beyond recognition. You were bruised, and your face was swollen. A crown of thorns was thrust upon your head, and you were bleeding. You were nailed to the cross, the nails into your flesh. Lord Jesus, in all that pain you loved us to the last breath. On the cross, you asked God to forgive us—we did not know what we were doing. You gave your mother to John so she would be provided for. You ministered to the thief on the cross—offered him paradise. Wow! You died. You rose from the dead. In that, I have hope. You now sit with the Father. I just have to believe, and let you change my life. Thank you, Lord Jesus.

"Holy Spirit, thank you too. You teach me. You teach me that God the Father loves me, that the Lord Jesus loved me enough to die for me and for all who will believe. Thank you, Holy Spirit. I come again and ask that you would teach me. Teach me the love, the will, the desire of the Father, and weave it into the fabric of my being. Teach me to love, to serve, to give. Teach me to bring it back to the Father and lay it at His feet that He would get the glory. Thank you, Holy Spirit.

"Father God, thank you for your Holy Bible and the precious gift of prayer.

"I am a sinner. Father, please forgive me for my sins. Help me to see the sin in my life, and give me the strength to walk away from sin. Help me to walk away from pride, arrogance, impatience, intolerance, lust, greed, envy, bitterness, anger, unforgivingness, fear, and anxiety. Teach me to love those I find difficult to love.

"Thank you for the blessings in my life. Thank you for my church, home, and family. I pray for this church. Thank you for my husband. Father, teach me to be the wife, friend, lover, and companion my husband needs. Help me to see his heart, the good he does. Teach me to honor him and to respect him, to seek his highest good. I pray that you would protect us, hold us close, and teach us to be faithful and fruitful. Lead us, guide us, and bless us for your kingdom and your glory.

"Thank you for our home. Please teach us to use this home for your glory. Teach us to grow in you, to love each other, to love those who come in, and to love those we meet when we go out. Thank you for the provisions you give us in this home. (I will name things like my toothbrush, the washer, and the dryer.)

"Thank you for work to do. Thank you for our children and grandchildren, our sisters and brothers, our nieces and nephews. I pray for them.

"Father, I now lift up our loved ones, our sisters, brothers, neighbors, coworkers, and ones who are sick. And I pray they would know Jesus. I pray your blessing, protection, and provision. I pray for a Christian witness and influence in their lives. I pray your healing, your peace, your comfort, and your strength in their lives. (At this point, I pray by name for each person I know.)

"Lord, I lift up my heart, my soul, and I pray this in Jesus's name. Amen."

Chapter 7

Go Forth and Make Disciples of Every Nation and Tribe

I have come to the end of my prayer. It is time to get up and go into the day. My desire is to live as if God were my God and Jesus was my Savior each and every day. My faith journey did not really begin in earnest until I prayed the "sinner's prayer." I prayed the prayer when I was listening to a radio program as I drove to work. I heard of a famous Christian author who decided to accept the principles and begin to live the Christian life. He felt that he would be a better person, and if he died and went to heaven, that would be even better. That was my thought as I prayed the sinner's prayer. He then went on to become a true believer. That is how it has happened with me. The more I have learned to love God, the more love I feel. I find a strength I have never known. Is it me? No. It is Jesus in me.

I also remember when I was first married to my husband and doing my usual "ask a million questions" thing, he kept saying to me, "What does the Bible say?" I finally got irritated and began reading my Bible. It is one of those moments that I am grateful for. First off, I was amazed I could read through the whole Bible. He had me read through it first. Now he likes to pick a book and read it slowly. I tend to read it through each year and do some sort of other study. Sometimes, I buy Bible study guides and that helps me a lot. Right now, my church has a study that I read each week and then we discuss in class. I am learning a new study and haven't got it down fully. This time, I pick a chapter and then I "diagram and dissect it." After that, I write down what I have learned—me and writing are always connected in some way.

I have never led someone in the sinner's prayer. I believe that each of us has a role in the work we do for the Lord. Some plant the seed. That may mean we live our life as if Jesus was our Savior and others see us live our lives. I see me in this role the most. Some may water the seed. That may be this book, a teacher, a minister. Some may harvest for the Lord, lead people to Jesus. I also believe that God is the one who does all these things in us. There is a Scripture that I love that goes something like, "We are all members in Christ. The hand is not more important than the foot." Each Christian has a role. I like that. I am not Billy Graham. I am not Michael Youseff or Joyce Meyers. My friend whom I took to the recovery group is an everyday woman. I am learning to be content with being a background person. Not everyone is a great speaker, minister, up front type of person.

One story I love is one I heard a while ago. Someone wrote to a newspaper complaining about all the sermons they heard. They could not remember most of them; so basically, what was the use? Another wrote in about how their wife of many years had made him many meals. He could not remember each meal through the years. Those meals did nourish his body and helped him to be healthy. The many sermons were the spiritual food that helped a Christian to grow strong. It was not one thing but many that helped them to grow.

There is one more story I love. It is about "Stone Soup." A poor man ran out of food. He took a pot, put water in it and some stones. He made a fire and put the pot on the fire. He was outside. People came by and then they would ask, "What are you making?" He replied, "Stone Soup." The people would go home and bring something back. Some brought vegetables; some, potatoes; some, meat; and others, seasonings. In the end, the man had food, and many others were able to eat as well.

Again, I see that we each bring something to the table, so to speak. Some are the flavoring and others are more substantive in bringing the message of good news: "For God so loved the world that He sent His only begotten Son, that whoever should believe in Him should not perish, but have everlasting life."

I have another thought. My husband grew up in a crazy family. Both parents were married three times. His mother died when he was five years old. His dad married within months of his mother's death. His dad had a college education. He chose to be a migrant worker. His dad was a scoundrel. He had no problem with coming up with schemes, cheating people, many times family members. People would be so very angry that they wanted to harm his dad. His dad would come home and tell the family to pack right away. They moved several times in a year. My husband went into the Marine Corps, was injured, and retired from service. He then went on to live a wild life. At times, he was downright scary. He met Jesus again. He had met Jesus as a child. He would get on a bus and go to church. He was lonely, and Jesus was in his heart. Jesus comforted him. As he came back to a faith walk, my husband grew. At times, he fell back. Jesus picked him up, dusted him off, and then sent him on his way again. My husband and I were on a mission trip a few years ago. We were learning how to do street evangelism. My husband—who looks very clean-cut now—would find people who had lots of tattoos, who were pierced every place, and who were very rough looking. My husband was sitting on benches talking to them about the love of Jesus. They were comfortable with my husband, and he was comfortable with them. He knows them in ways I can't understand.

For me, I tend to have a heart for people dealing with abuse. I know how it feels to not have any control in your life. I know the anger you feel.

My "survivors of abuse" group has helped me as much as I have helped them. Whenever I go back to Michigan, I attend this group. Again, we all have a person we can relate to, and to me, that is an opportunity to reach out and to love as I have been loved.

At this point, I'd like to introduce the sinner's prayer. I believe it is important to recognize that we are all sinners. Once I acknowledged that, I found myself being able to grow; prior to that, I had a hard time letting go of anger, hurt, and many other problems.

"Lord God, forgive me for I am a sinner. (You may want to name your sins.) Please forgive me. Help me to walk away from sin. I ask that you, Lord Jesus, would come to live within my heart. I ask you to be my Savior. I believe, Lord Jesus, that you are the Son of God and sent here ultimately dying on the cross to atone for my sins and make me right with God."

It is also important to tell someone when you have done this. I think it is important because we need to admit to ourselves and to someone else. It is like cementing, making it important, a declaration if you will, that this is truly the way you want to be now.

I was also baptized recently. This was important to me. I went under the water, and my sins were washed away. As I came up, I was a new creation in Christ. That symbolism helps me to realize the gift of salvation. It makes my walk in some way more real.

As you ask for Jesus to be in you, the Holy Spirit will come into your life as well. He is a helper and a comforter.

I pray that this book helps you and encourages you.

Index

LaVergne, TN USA
12 August 2010
192998LV00004B/35/P